Amazing Histories

THE AMAZING HISTORY OF
FASHION

BY KESHA GRANT

CAPSTONE PRESS
a capstone imprint

Published by Capstone Press, an imprint of Capstone.
1710 Roe Crest Drive, North Mankato, Minnesota 56003
capstonepub.com

Library of Congress Cataloging-in-Publication Data
Names: Grant, Kesha, author.
Title: The amazing history of fashion / by Kesha Grant.
Description: North Mankato, Minnesota : Spark, an imprint of Capstone, [2023] | Series: Amazing histories | Includes bibliographical references and index. | Audience: Ages 9–11 | Audience: Grades 4–6 | Summary: "How we dress today looks a lot different than it did in the past. From clothing as a status symbol to the invention of denim and rise of blue jeans, the history of fashion is full of unusual, amazing, and fascinating facts. Learn more about how people throughout history have used fashion in everyday life."—Provided by publisher.
Identifiers: LCCN 2022024539 (print) | LCCN 2022024540 (ebook) | ISBN 9781669011804 (hardcover) | ISBN 9781669011750 (paperback) | ISBN 9781669011767 (pdf) | ISBN 9781669011781 (kindle edition)
Subjects: LCSH: Fashion—History—Juvenile literature. | Clothing and dress—History—Juvenile literature.
Classification: LCC GT518 .G73 2023 (print) | LCC GT518 (ebook) | DDC 391.009—dc23/eng/20220525
LC record available at https://lccn.loc.gov/2022024539
LC ebook record available at https://lccn.loc.gov/2022024540

Editorial Credits
Editor: Alison Deering; Designer: Jaime Willems; Media Researcher: Donna Metcalf; Production Specialist: Tori Abraham

Image Credits
Alamy: ClassicStock, 20; Getty Images: Alessandra Benedetti, 9, Ann Ronan Pictures, 7, Bob Bird/Mirrorpix, 27, Daniel Karmann/picture alliance, 17, Fotosearch, 12, Hulton Archive, 18, Scott Gries, 19, Sophie Bassouls, 21, Benjamin B, 16; Shutterstock: conzorb, cover top left, Delpixel, 10, DFree, 25, Everett Collection, cover left, Fascinadora, 29, Filip Fuxa, 22, Gorodenkoff, 28, gowithstock, 5, Helena Ohman, cover right, Klahan, 15, LightField Studios, cover middle, Linda Hughes Photography, 24, Macrovector, 4, 13, 26, miniwide, 6, 8, 23, Xinovap, 14

TABLE OF CONTENTS

Words in **BOLD** are in the glossary.

WHAT'S IN YOUR CLOSET?

Your style says a lot about you. That hasn't changed throughout history. Fashion has always shown us the amazing ways people lived.

ANCIENT
FASHIONS

Ancient Egypt was hot! People used fashion to stay cool. Men and women wore skirts and dresses made of **linen**. They also changed outfits up to four times a day!

Until the age of six, kids wore no clothes at all. But they still rocked jewelry, just like Mom and Dad.

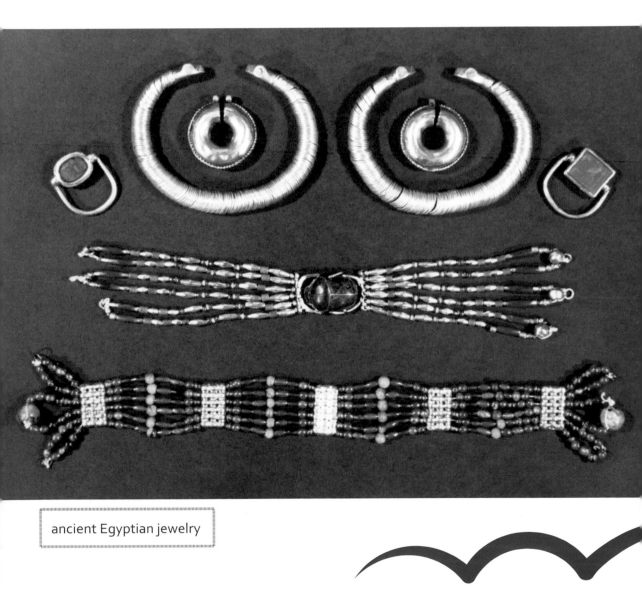

ancient Egyptian jewelry

Ancient Rome

In ancient Rome, the rich wore silk robes from China. Royals even paid extra to have their clothes dyed purple. One pound of purple dye cost three pounds of gold! That's about $91,000 today!

Purple robes showed wealth in ancient Rome.

Regular Romans weren't as flashy. Their robes came in dull colors. Most were made of wool.

FASHION
INVENTIONS

Indigo plants are turned into dye.

Enslaved people in North America had a big impact on fashion. They turned **indigo** plants into a blue dye. The process took a lot of time and effort.

The dye was popular with wealthy families in North America and Europe. They paid top dollar for indigo blue clothing.

Two gold miners wear Levi jeans outside of the Last Chance Mine in California in 1882.

The Rise of Denim

Today, blue jeans are everywhere. But denim wasn't popular in the United States until the 1850s. Levi Strauss started selling the pants in his store during the Gold Rush. The tough fabric was perfect for miners.

Jacob Davis made the pants stronger. He added **rivets** around the pockets. These tiny bits of metal helped prevent ripping.

DID YOU KNOW?

The first blue jeans were only meant for men. Women didn't start wearing these trendy bottoms until 1934.

FOOT
FASHIONS

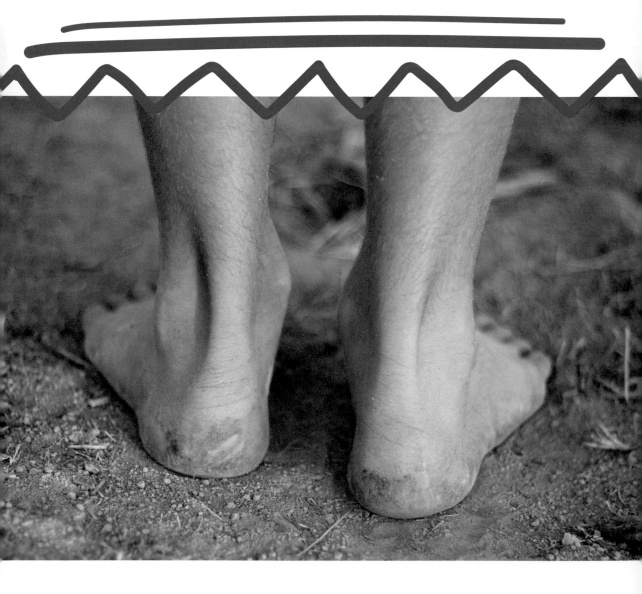

Tree sap flows from a rubber tree.

Some people living in the Amazon rain forests don't wear cloth shoes. They coat their feet with rubber tree **sap.** The sap provides a layer of protection once it hardens. People can move across the rainforest on "rubber feet."

Family Feud

Two of the most popular shoe brands are related! In the 1920s, German brothers Adolf "Adi" Dassler and Rudolf Dassler teamed up. They started sewing sneakers in their parents' laundry room.

In 1948, the brothers split. No one knows exactly why. Adi went on to found Adidas. Rudolf started Puma. The brands are rivals to this day.

A statue of Adolf Dassler sits outside an Adidas office building.

STYLISH
REBELS

Josephine Baker wears one of her famous outfits—a feathered dress.

In the 1920s, stylish rebels took center stage. Performer Josephine Baker was ahead of her time with many trends. She wore flapper dresses, feathered outfits—even a banana miniskirt!

Baker's impact can still be seen today. Beyoncé, Rihanna, and more have worn outfits inspired by Baker.

Beyoncé performs in 2006 in an outfit inspired by Baker.

Black Is Beautiful

Before the 1960s, fashion magazines showed beauty one way. Models had light skin, blue eyes, and straight, blond hair.

Black models showed a different version of beauty in the 1960s and 1970s.

DID YOU KNOW?

Angela Davis was a fashionable Civil Rights activist. She sported jeans, miniskirts, and sunglasses, and an afro that was a symbol of Black pride.

That changed in 1962. Photographer Kwame Brathwaite put on a fashion show. He used Black models. They showed off brown skin, curly afros, full lips, and curvy bodies. The show proved beauty comes in many colors.

GLOBAL
STYLES

Saris come in many different colors and designs.

There's an outfit for every occasion. In India, that's a **sari**. The word means "strip of cloth." Women have worn these for more than 5,000 years.

A sari is a work of art. The cloths are full of color and design. One sari can be styled more than 100 different ways!

Kente Cloth

A spider inspired one of Africa's most popular fashions! Kentes are colorful woven cloths. They are decorated with special designs.

Legend says two brothers learned to make the cloths by watching a spider weave a special web. At first, only kings wore kente. But now anyone can enjoy it.

FASHION
TODAY

Streetwear is about comfort and style.
Surfers and skaters made this style popular
in the 1980s. They wore **graphic** tees.

Hip-hop artists put their own twist on
this look. They made baggy jeans popular.

Streetwear ruled in the 1980s.

Care What You Wear

Fast fashion gives us trendy clothes quickly.

But it can also be bad for the environment.

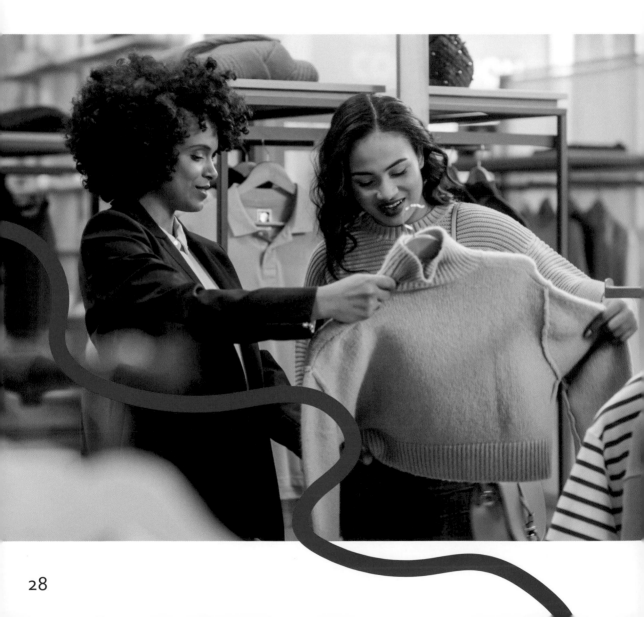

Some designers are trying to change that. They make **sustainable** fashions. They use recycled clothing, organic cotton, and other materials. These styles are better for the planet and the people who make them.

GLOSSARY

ancient (AYN-shunt)—from a long time ago

graphic (GRAF-ik)—having drawings or designs

indigo (IN-di-goh)—a plant that produces a deep-blue dye

linen (LIN-uhn)—a cloth made from the flax plant

rivet (RIV-it)—a strong metal bolt that is used to fasten something together

sap (SAP)—a sticky, watery fluid that flows inside trees

sari (SAH-ree)—a long piece of cloth that is wrapped around a woman's body

sustainable (suh-STAY-nuh-buhl)—a method of using resources so that the resource is not damaged or destroyed

READ MORE

Albee, Sarah. *Why'd They Wear That?: Fashion as the Mirror of History*. Washington. D.C.: National Geographic Kids, 2015.

Sedlackova, Jana. *The Complete Book of Fashion History: A Stylish Journey Through History and the Ultimate Guide For Being Fashionable In Every Era*. Mission Viejo, CA: Walter Foster Jr., 2017.

Slee, Natasha. *Planet Fashion: 100 Years of Fashion History*. London, England: Quarto Publishing Group, 2019.

INTERNET SITES

DK findout!: Fashion
dkfindout.com/us/history/fashion

Ducksters: History for Kids
ducksters.com/history

History for Kids
historyforkids.net

INDEX

photo credit: Malcolm Grant

ABOUT THE AUTHOR

Kesha Grant is an educator, researcher, and children's book author. Her first book, *Women in the Civil Rights Movement: A Scholastic True Book*, was released in 2020. She holds a Master's degree in Education and a Master's of Fine Arts degree in Creative Writing. She blends these two specialties together to write true accounts of unsung heroes whose stories never made it into the history books but definitely deserve to be there. She lives in Atlanta, Georgia, with her husband, children, and two very fat guinea pigs named Zuko and Boba.